THE *DANGERS* of "FREE TRADE"

John M. Culbertson

21st Century Press
P.O. Box 5010, Madison, WI 53705

Copyright © 1985 by John M. Culbertson.
All rights reserved.
Printed in the United States of America.

ISBN 0-918357-03-9 (pbk., trade)
ISBN 0-918357-04-7 (pbk., text)

21st Century Press, P. O. Box 5010, Madison, Wis. 53705

CONTENTS

1   The New Threat of International Trade   1
2   The New International Wage-Competition   15
3   Wage-Competition and Its Implications   21
4   Further Effects of Economic Merger   32
5   Achieving Beneficial International Trade   38

John M. Culbertson is Professor of Economics at University of Wisconsin-Madison. He has been an economist with The Board of Governors of the Federal Reserve System, consultant to the Federal Reserve Bank of St. Louis, the Subcommittee on International Finance of the House Banking and Currency Committee, and the USAID Mission to Bolivia. He also toured Southeast Asia for the U. S. Information Agency and lectured on monetary economics at University of Paris. He is the author of five earlier books.

1

THE NEW THREAT OF INTERNATIONAL TRADE

The United States is losing many rewarding industries and jobs to other countries. Other high-income Western nations have the same problem. The industries and jobs are shifting to countries that have lower costs, which mainly reflect lower wage rates and standards of living. The output is largely shipped back to be sold in the markets of the high-wage nations. The high-wage nations thus face a loss of their rewarding industries and jobs, and of their prospects for future economic development, while suffering large deficits in their international trade.

To what kind of future does this process lead? The "normal economic adjustment" to this situation will be worsening unemployment in the high-income nations, which leads to a drop in their wage rates and their standard of living. These events are already under way.

Recent changes in the world economic situation have thrown the workers of the high-income nations into a new kind of competition with those of efficient low-wage nations. All countries now have access to the same technology and management methods. Thus, all workers now are competing on equal terms. In this new situation, unregulated international trade tends to

The Dangers of "Free Trade"

equalize wage rates in different nations. In a world that is economically merged by unregulated international trade, no basis exists for United States workers to receive wage rates that are many times higher than those of Japanese, Koreans, Taiwanese, Chinese. Under "free trade," the required "adjustment" is a decline in the wage level and standard of living of the United States and other high-income nations to equality with that of these other nations—which will rise somewhat, but not to near the recent Western level.

But the people of the United States and other high-income nations are not expecting a great decline in their wage rates and standard of living. To the economist contemplating abstract theories, such a decline may seem a desirable result of the operation of "the free market." But the peoples who lose a way of life they have known for generations will not take the matter so lightly. The undermining, and the likely demoralization and disorganization, of the nations that for many decades have been world leaders and pattern-setters would place human affairs in an uncertain position.

Moreover, the prospect of such economic merger of nations through international trade raises the question whether it is desirable from the viewpoint of mankind in general for international wage-competition in this overpopulated world to pull all nations down to a lowest-common-denominator standard of living. In such a world, the effects of the severe and worsening world overpopulation would be imposed on all nations, on those that have limited their populations as much as those whose populations are out of control. Within such a "world as a population commune," no nation would have the power or capability of achieving a high standard of living and a preserved environment. The nations that do not control their overpopulation will set the pattern that is imposed on all nations. This is essentially an if-any-of-us-fail-we-all-fail economic structure for the world. It embodies the enormous failure-producing power of the commune.

The successful national economies operate under the opposite kind of structure, the if-any-of-us-succeed-we-all-succeed structure. This preserves separate—rather than merged—economic units. These units retain control of their affairs and can follow different policies, can generate diverse "experiments." The most successful of these experiments then are copied by others and come to prevail. This is the basic structure of the "natural selection" that created the world of living things. This if-any-of-us-succeed-we-all-succeed structure was the framework for the past advances of human life. It is the pattern of competition among firms in successful economies. The question thus is raised whether the wage-competition and the nation-merging or communalizing effects of unregulated international trade in today's world are not an unparalleled threat to human well-being.[1]

These implications of recent economic events are not widely understood in the United States. A reason for this is that the recently fashionable version of economics, the "neoclassical theoretical economics," does not provide an economic analysis of the effects of the structures and processes that actually are operating. Rather, it provides models and theories that derive from a set of assumptions. These assumptions reflect a political faith or ideology. This is a faith in, as Adam Smith put it, "natural harmony" under "natural liberty," the conception that things naturally work out for the best, without planning or guidance by government, when each person and business firm pursues its own profit. Those thinking within this theoretical framework do not notice that under the new conditions that now exist, economic *laissez faire* and "free trade" lead to an economic merging of nations and to an if-any-of-us-fail-we-all-fail structuring of human life.

[1] A more detailed and comprehensive treatment of this subject is given in Culbertson, *International Trade and the Future of the West* (Madison, Wis.: 21st Century Press, 1984). See also, *The United States in a Changing World Economy: The Case for an Integrated Domestic and International Commercial Policy*, Staff Report, House Committee on Energy and Commerce (Washington, D. C.: U. S. Government Printing Office, 1983). A major earlier work dealing with the subject in a different historical context is Friedrich List, *The National System of Political Economy* (Fairfield, N. J.: Augustus M. Kelley, 1977, first published in 1841).

4 The Dangers of "Free Trade"

A problem of such enormous implications as the rapidly changing patterns of international trade and industry seems to call for realistic analysis of the situation that actually exists and the implications of the processes that actually are occurring. The successful sciences that have made great achievements in understanding how the world works and in permitting the realization of human goals have worked in this way. To interpret such a problem in terms of a theory that reflects a set of political preconceptions rather than cause-and-effect analysis of actual structures and processes does not seem at all satisfactory. To consider this complex and all-important subject in terms of the "'free trade' is good—'protectionism' is bad" sloganism that dominates recent United States discussion seems grotesquely inadequate.

"THE DEINDUSTRIALIZATION OF AMERICA"

In the past twenty years, the United States has experienced an accelerating exodus of its major industries, and a growing excess of its imports over its exports. The flow into the United States in 1984 of goods produced in other countries was more than $100 billion greater than the flow of goods produced in the United States and sold in other countries. If U. S. trade had been in balance, so an additional $100 billion worth of the goods bought were produced in the U. S. rather than in other countries, a great many more Americans would have had jobs.

Even more important, in giving up important industries—turning them over to other countries—the nation is giving away its economic future. The jobs and the incomes that Americans will have in the future will depend on the industries the nation has operating. Lost industries are a lost basis for future economic development, for future technological advances, for development of front-running skills and productive powers.

The industries that have shifted partly or entirely to other nations in the past twenty years include steel, automobiles, machinery, textiles, clothing, shoes, radios, television sets, and other electrical equipment, cameras, optical equipment, photographic film, tractors and farm equipment, aluminum, glassware, shipbuilding, mining. In 1985, agriculture—widely assumed to be the unassailable citadel of American productivity—began to be undersold by foreign output of grains and was in serious trouble, and oil refineries were being closed down under foreign competition.[2]

One initial reaction to the foreign underselling of the United States steel and automobile industries was that it reflected only poor management in those industries and a slippage in their "productivity." But it is difficult now to argue that the shift of so many industries and jobs reflects the simultaneous failure of the American managements of *all of those industries*—the more so when the same thing is happening to European industries.

The general story is not the failure of American managements or a loss of "productivity" of American workers but the effects of a much broader force. Low-wage nations that earlier were not in a position to challenge Western production using Western machinery and production methods have gained the ability to do so. Their lower labor costs enable them to undersell American production in many industries. Other contributing factors are subsidization of their exports by their governments, and cost-saving from avoiding regulations that apply to U. S. production. Such is the story that emerges from a case-by-case consideration of the recent shifts in production and jobs.[3]

It sometimes is argued that the industries the United States has been losing are only old-fashioned or second-class indus-

---

[2] It was to be expected that the United States would recede from the unique position of world industrial dominance it temporarily had after the Second World War, before the war-damaged nations had rebuilt their economies. But recent events have not comprised a return to a prewar "normal" but a movement toward a radically new situation.

[3] Of course, other factors also are operating. The international value of the dollar being pushed to unreasonable heights by the flow of foreign funds into the United States surely contributed to the undercutting of U. S. production by foreign production. But quantitatively this factor is small in relation to the wage-differential factor. And it is to be noted that though a major decline in the value of the dollar would help make American industry internationally competitive, it would do this *by reducing American real wage rates and the American standard of living.*

tries, which we should be glad to turn over to "less-developed nations." The idea is that new, more demanding and more rewarding, industries will appear to provide higher-income jobs for the displaced American workers. But this view also does not fit the facts. Many of the industries that have been lost are technically advanced, and have promising futures. New "advanced" industries that will provide attractive jobs for millions of Americans have not appeared on the scene, and there seems no reason to expect them. Nor, if they did, is there any reason to believe that the United States—at its present wage rates and standard of living—would be more able to meet Japanese, Taiwanese, South Korean competition in such new industries than in the industries it has been losing.

In seeking to find the meaning of recent events, it is important to remember that this kind of loss of industries and jobs— or "deindustrialization"[4]—is not limited to the United States. It is affecting all high-income nations, even the industrial leader and powerhouse, Germany, as well as France, Sweden, Belgium. Even Japan, which has been the recent leader and pattern-setter in gaining desirable industries from other nations, has been finding its industries threatened by lower-cost competition from South Korea—and South Korea is becoming concerned over competition from countries with still lower wage rates.

The loss of industries and jobs to foreign competition and the common knowledge that the lower foreign labor costs were the major basis of this has put pressure on United States workers to forego their accustomed wage increases, and even to accept pay cuts. Recent years have seen an "unprecedented wave of wage cuts and freezes."[5] Since 1979, one sixth of United States union members have accepted labor contracts that freeze or reduce wages and fringe benefits or alter work rules. Average

---

[4] This term was popularized and the situation to which it refers was graphically described in Barry Bluestone and Bennett Harrison, *The Deindustrialization of America* (New York: Basic Books, 1982).

[5] "Union Settlements and Aggregate Wage Behavior in the 1980s," *Federal Reserve Bulletin*, Dec. 1984, p. 856.

wage increases in union settlements dropped from about 10 percent in 1981 to 2½ percent in 1983 and 1984. The effects of low-wage foreign competition were reflected also in the shifting composition of the available jobs. Attractive, high-paid jobs were eliminated. Those who lost these jobs usually had to accept lower incomes to find other jobs. Not only production workers but white-collar employees and executives who had looked forward confidently to a life career with a major company found themselves jobless. It is estimated that more than 1 million white-collar workers lost their positions because of plant shutdowns or job cutbacks.[6] The job-loss and the downward pressure on wage rates and living standards that characterize the declining economy already have begun to hit the United States.

In the 1960s, some believed that "economic development" or "economic growth" would provide the high-income, "developed" nations with continued—indeed, automatic—progress, while the "less-developed" nations would enjoy rapid, catch-up advancement so that all nations would become affluent. But it is obvious that the rise of those low-income countries that recently have rapidly industrialized has been based largely on their underselling of the production of high-wage nations and taking over their industries. New rewarding industries have not appeared that could provide comparable jobs for the millions of people in high-wage nations who lost rewarding jobs because of being undersold by low-wage foreign labor. Neither did such a thing happen in the past when nations lost their major industries and went into economic decline. Those theories of "economic growth" seem to have been unrealistic in not recognizing that the gaining of the rewarding industries of the times by one nation implies the loss of them by another—that one nation's "industrialization" can imply another nation's "deindustrialization."

[6] See "'Suddenly, the World Doesn't Care If You Live or Die'," *Business Week*, February 4, 1985, pp. 96, 98. Recent job losses reflected other factors along with international wage-competition, but the great factor causing job-loss and the changing environment of labor negotiations seems to be the inescapable reality and spreading influence of international wage-competition.

It is not, thus, unreasonable to ask: "What kind of policies and what structure of international trade are needed to assure that Pittsburgh, Chicago, and Detroit do not become industrial ghost towns, empty and quiet, their people moved away as the opportunities to earn a living disappeared, as their products were undersold by production from low-wage nations? What policies will prevent the United States from finding its production undersold by imported goods, losing the rewarding industries of the times, slipping into economic decline, and becoming only a shadow of what it once had been?"

"INTERNATIONAL TRADE," SOME CLARIFICATIONS

The term, "international trade," sounds as if it means "trade between nations." But trade between *nations, as nations*, would be trade that is arranged between the governments of the nations. After all, its government is the agency that acts on behalf of *the nation*.

International trade of the kind labeled "free trade" involves the opposite situation. This is trade across the boundaries of the nation that the government plays no part in directing or guiding. In "free trade," the government, or *the nation*, is not "free" to do anything whatever. Private firms and individuals, acting in their own interests, are "free" to do as they wish. What they are "free of," of course, is action by the government, or by *the nation*.

Thus, one must keep in mind that "international trade" does not mean "trade between nations, as nations" but "trade that crosses a national boundary," or "boundary-crossing trade." And "free trade" refers to the situation in which traders (who may be citizens and residents of any country) have the "freedom" to engage in any kind of boundary-crossing transactions—while workers, environmentalists, the general public, acting through their government have *no freedom* to define any rules for the activities of the traders.

In the case of *trade between nations* there would be some basis for arguing that the nations involved must benefit from the trade, for otherwise they would not agree to engage in it.

But in the case of *trade across national boundaries carried out by individuals and firms in pursuit of profit* there is no basis for asserting that the *nations* benefit. This distinction is not always kept clear.

One may be misled by the way "freedom" and "free" are used in connection with international trade. Proponents of "free trade" often treat "freedom" as if it were a simple matter of more versus less. More "freedom" is better than less "freedom." "Free trade" means more "freedom." Therefore, "free trade" is the best arrangement. The words settle the matter. No knowledge or analysis is needed.

But a policy of "free trade" involves implicitly saying to potential traders of all countries, "You may engage in any transactions you wish across our boundaries. Our government will not limit your actions, whatever their effects." This implies saying to the nation's workers, "No actions can be taken to keep you from being thrown into wage-competition with the workers of low-wage, overpopulated nations." Granting "free trade" thus does not simply add to total human freedom. It grants privileges to traders at the expense of taking away rights from others. In such cases, it is necessary to consider not only what is given, but also what is taken away.

Another important implication of "free trade" is brought out by noting its similarity in effects to "free migration." "Free migration" implies that the people of a low-wage nation would be "free" to move to a nation that had high wages—where they could get jobs by undercutting the local workers and still be better off than they had been in their own country. A policy of "free migration" thus would mean that the people of a high-wage nation were not "free" to keep their jobs and preserve their high standard of living. To do this they must be able to prevent an influx of people from low-wage nations. It is the one "freedom" against the other. To assert a "freedom" of people to migrate is to deny any "freedom" of people to maintain a high standard of living against an influx of outsiders.

"Free trade" is the same kind of case. The movement of goods across national boundaries has many of the same effects as the movement of people. It does not much matter, for example, whether people move from low-wage Mexico to the United States to get jobs under "free migration" or whether the industries and the jobs move from the United States to low-wage Mexico—which they can do if the output can be shipped back for sale in the U. S. market under "free trade." Thus, the United States wage rate and standard of living could be undercut in the same way by "free trade" as by "free migration"—and recently has been under pressure from both forces.

Either "free migration" or "free trade" potentially prevents any nation from achieving a high standard of living in a world in which other nations, for whatever reason, have large numbers of unemployed or impoverished people. The question must be raised whether the "freedom" of the people of a nation to defend its standard of living is not more important than the "freedom" of traders to profit from shipping goods across national boundaries.

THE "FREE TRADE" DOCTRINE VERSUS RECENT EVIDENCE

Because of its great influence and the support it recently has received from *laissez faire* economics, it is important to point out that the free-trade doctrine is not supported by recent events:

1. A basic idea of the free-trade view is that unregulated boundary-crossing trade is automatically beneficial to both of the nations involved. In recent experience, many shifts in trade patterns have benefitted one nation at the expense of another. On investigation, this proves to be true also in the past. There is no explanation as to how deals governed only by their profitability to private parties can be necessarily beneficial to the *nations* involved.

2. The recent great changes in patterns of trade and the location of industries cannot be justified as moving toward an ideal situation that is defined by "economic theory." The idealized "optimal equilibrium positions" of theoretical economics assume that basic causal factors such as population, technology, and level of living standards are fixed and unchanging. In the present case, all of these factors are not fixed, but are affected

by the evolutionary changes that are occurring. Thus, this economic theory cannot define the outcome of the processes now under way. To do this requires an economic analysis that takes account of all of the interactions among causal factors, including changes in population, standards of living, and applicable technology.

3. The free-trade doctrine traditionally asserts that low foreign wage rates cannot undercut the economy of a high-wage nation. "The principle of comparative advantage" says that differences in the general levels of wage rates in different nations have no effect on trade (only "comparative costs," not "absolute costs," matter). Recent events dramatically show that absolute costs of production and absolute wage rates are what govern the shift of industries between nations. It is mainly low foreign wage rates that are undercutting American production and jobs. It is competition in cutting their absolute costs that forces firms to move their operations to low-wage nations.

4. Boundary-crossing trade causes not only such wage-competition but also a destructive competition in cutting costs by reducing other kinds of standards. Production moves to countries where firms can avoid the costs of anti-pollution actions, of worker-protection devices and procedures, of resource-conservation requirements, of safety equipment and procedures. International competition for industries and jobs tends to reduce all such standards, as well as wage rates, to a lowest-common-denominator level.

5. Governments that are forced to compete against one another to hold industries and jobs for their people will find that this competition prevents them from doing anything about environmental destruction, safety, low wage rates caused by overpopulation, any form of regulation of business. Governments also will have to compete in keeping their own costs and taxes low as an element in the international competition. In this situation, national governments will no longer possess the kind of powers they have exercised in the past, or the powers needed to protect the interests of their peoples. In natural-harmony ideology this would be no problem, for government is hardly needed. But it seems clear that effective national governments

are the only agencies that can deal with many present-day problems.

6. The theoretical economics used to justify free trade does not provide causal explanations of events such as are demanded by modern scientific thinking. Rather, it rests on conventionalized assumptions that are carried forward from a pre-scientific era when they were thought to represent "self-evident truths." Experience and critical thought have disclosed that such "self-evident truths" are usually mere prejudices or wishes. The output of the voluminous "economic research" based on this theory is governed by its assumptions and thus does not provide valid information about the actual workings of economies. What is needed is to put aside unrealistic economic theories and docrines that have political origins, and to develop a realistic view of the implications of recent events by applying the valid tools of economic analysis.

WAYS OF STRUCTURING INTERNATIONAL TRADE

Recent popular discussion of international trade commonly assumes a choice of "free trade" *or* "protectionism." As we have seen, "free trade" eliminates the "freedom" of the nation's workers to protect their standard of living, and of the nation to defend itself against reductions in its standard of living caused by international wage-competition. It also eliminates the ability of mankind to escape the if-anyone-fails-we-all-fail structure of the world as a population commune. It seems, thus, that "free-tradism" is a dangerous affliction.

"Protectionism" is usually defined as a government policy of offering tariff or quota protection against imports to any industry or labor union that asks for it, that is, serving private interests without any regard for the public interest. Obviously, this kind of policy also has little to recommend it.[7]

---

[7] But the term "protectionism" also is sometimes applied to any and all departures from unregulated international trade. This is a misleading use of language. It implies that all government regulation or guidance of international trade is done at the behest of special interests and in violation of the public interest. Such an assertion can in no way be supported by the facts.

In truth, experience shows that there are many kinds of policies toward international trade that can be considered other than "free trade" and "protectionism." Japan and the other nations that recently have achieved rapid economic advancement have guided the pattern of their international trade and industrial development in an effort to gain the most promising industries. This kind of policy has been very rewarding to some countries. But for all nations to engage in a no-holds-barred struggle to win away from one another the desired industries of the times would be a wasteful and conflict-causing arrangement. What more constructive arrangements for international trade are available for consideration?

The working of the successful economy is not based on a pattern of such conflict, or on anarchistic "freedom" of firms to do anything, or on the use of government policy to further private interests. Is there not a way of extending to international trade the constructive structure within which successful economies achieve their wonders of organized production? For international trade to apply the structure and the constructive interaction that drives the successful economy, how would it have to be set up?

The central theme of successful economies is *mutuality*. The economy is driven by mutually beneficial deals that are struck among individuals, families, and firms—all within a necessary framework of laws and rules. In this kind of system, each person, family, firm is capable of pursuing its own interests, of setting its goals and pursuing them. This implies that they must not be communalized and thereby deprived of the power of independent action. The person acts for himself or herself in deciding what deals to accept. The family acts through its chosen members. The firm acts through its officials who are given authority to act on its behalf.

To extend this logic to the higher level of organization requires that *the nation act through its government to make deals with other nations that will serve the interests of the nation and its people.* The pattern of mutuality, of reciprocal benefit, of independent choice and responsibility that governs the successful economy thus is carried to the level of economic organization of the nation.

Whatever arrangements for international trade may prove to be beneficial in particular cases, the starting point for thinking about trade across national boundaries thus seems to be (1) that it must be based on mutually beneficial economic dealings between *nations*, and (2) that this can be done only through the guidance or management of international trade by governments. There is no other way to preserve the needed powers and capacities of nations, and to extend to trade across national boundaries that principle of mutual benefit that governs the effective economy.

Thus, the starting point for thinking about international trade is not "'free trade' or 'protectionism'," but "mutually beneficial trade between nations." The recent pattern of international trade has not been mutually beneficial. It is undercutting the economies and the standards of living of the United States and the West. The situation requires a serious and realistic rethinking of policy toward international trade.

2

THE NEW INTERNATIONAL WAGE-COMPETITION

How is it that international wage-competition now threatens to pull all nations down to a low standard of living when such a thing does not seem to have happened in the past? The answer is that altered circumstances have revolutionized the workings and the effects of international trade. International trade thus has very different effects now than it did in the nineteenth century, or before the Second World War.

In the past, the people of the high-income nations and those of the low-income nations were largely noncompeting groups. The workers of low-wage countries could not take away the jobs of workers in high-wage nations, even though they would work diligently for very much less. Firms then did not compete at cutting costs by moving industries from high-wage to low-wage nations—as they so strikingly have in recent years. It is important to understand the factors that have brought about this new situation, and have given international trade a new kind of meaning.

THE ELIMINATION OF PROTECTIONS AGAINST WORLD WAGE-COMPETITION

The dedication to "free trade" and the great efforts to reduce "barriers to trade" that have characterized the postwar period were not typical of earlier times. The attempt of the United States to move the world toward unregulated international trade was something new to the world. Adam Smith's doctrine of "free trade" has been around for a long time, but it has never been so in favor with economists as recently. In earlier times it had little effect on the policies of governments, which mainly reflected the view that international trade is not automatically self-regulating, so the nation that values its future must see that it does not lose its rewarding industries or import more than it exports.

International trade commonly was managed or steered by governments, in various ways and to varying degrees. A major goal was to prevent the undercutting of the nation's rewarding industries by foreign competition. It was traditional to try to prevent the production methods and trade secrets of successful industries from becoming available to foreigners. The undercutting of a valued local industry by foreign production might lead to a tariff or quota to protect the threatened industry. The recent endeavor actually to bring about "free trade"—trusting to the natural workings of "the market" to replace those lost industries and jobs—this is a new kind of undertaking.

One form of government management of international trade and the international location of industry was the colonial system. The trade of a colony was managed by the colonial power so its industries would be complementary to, rather than competitive with, its own industries. Colonialism was valued as providing the colonial power with a favorable source of imports of raw materials and simple goods and with a market for its advanced manufactured goods. The colonial power thus would not think of permitting its rewarding industries to be won away from it by its colony, however cheap the labor the colony was able to provide. The operation of this system of management of international trade kept a large part of the earth's population from wage-competition with the Western nations. But the colonial system no longer exists to prevent India and the many other populous ex-colonies from entering into international competition in whatever industries they choose.

Until recently, the local cultures, customs, and religions of many areas still posed substantial barriers to Western-style factory production. In some areas, such as parts of Africa and the Middle East, that still is true. But the spread of a world uniculture based on Western ideas has largely removed these barriers to world economic merger in most areas of the world. It would have been difficult to imagine GM setting up a state-of-the-art factory in the China or the Korea of fifty years ago, but now such things do not have to be imagined. They are commonplace.

Until recently, most other areas were unable to compete on equal terms with Western production because of their lack of technical know-how, capital, organizing and managerial skills and experience, and links to Western markets. Beginning only in recent decades, all of these essential and difficult-to-create requirements of efficient, modern production are available through the great powers of multinational corporations. These giant, world-spanning organizations, in some cases not closely tied to any particular nation, basically change the world situation with regard to the international location of industries and the pattern of international trade. Their existence implies that areas and workers that in the past would have been quite incapable of posing a competitive threat to high-wage Western workers are now able to engage in wage-competition with Western workers *on equal terms.* That is a revolutionary change in the shape of the world.

The achievements in a number of low-wage nations of very efficient, realistic, and economically ambitious governments have supplemented the role of multinational corporations, in some countries made them superfluous. The very skillful and effective collaborative work of government and local firms created the new organizational structure that was needed for the local workers to enter into competition with Western workers.

The efficient government planning and administration that underlay the Japanese "economic miracle" was a remarkable achievement. It was well copied by the other Asian nations that have provided the great economic success stories of recent decades. These political accomplishments also are something new in the world.

Political and ideological barriers that earlier sufficed to keep billions of workers from wage-competition with the West seem to be easing or disappearing. Chairman Mao's ideology kept China's billion people out of wage-competition with the West, but the rapidly changing Chinese economic policy of the 1980s abruptly altered the situation. The political ideas that severely limited India's industrial development and wage-competition also appear to be changing. In these two nations, nearly half the world's people may now be ready to enter into a game from which they earlier had been excluded by the political beliefs of their leaders.

These changes in circumstances create a radically new economic structure of the world. Unrestricted and unregulated private trade across national boundaries now has quite different effects than it would have had in the past. What might have passed as "free trade" in the 1800s—though there was little pretense then that "free trade" prevailed—would have had nothing like the effects of "free trade" in the late twentieth century.

THE INCREASED SCOPE AND POWER OF INTERNATIONAL WAGE-COMPETITION

The drastic reductions in the costs and delays of shipping goods, moving people, and communicating have brought a revolutionary increase in the scope and potential effects of international wage-competition. Jet aircraft, supertankers, instantaneous communications and data-transmission imply that a factory or an office in a distant part of the world is no longer out of touch, or out of control. It now is quite feasible for a firm to shift its production from Michigan to the Phillippines or

Taiwan—and to ship the output quickly and cheaply back to sell in U. S. markets. The revolutionary changes in communications and computing raise now the possibility of making paperwork, and some kinds of "service industries" such as insurance, able to shift to foreign nations to seek low-wage labor. New technological achievements have shrunk the world. Peoples that in earlier times would have been quite unable to engage in wage-competition with Western workers because of the time and the cost of distance now can compete as if they were right next door.

THE POPULATION EXPLOSION AND INTERNATIONAL WAGE-COMPETITION

The population explosion of recent decades—which has added 2 billion people and doubled world population since the Second World War—has enormously increased the pool of low-wage labor available for wage-competition with Western workers. This is true not only in absolute numbers of available low-wage workers but also in relative terms. Population has grown most rapidly, and continues to grow most rapidly, in low-wage nations—their rapid population growth being a major reason, in some cases *the* reason, why they *are* low-wage nations.

When international wage-competition and the shift of industries and jobs from high-wage to low-wage areas works to equalize world wage rates, the level of the equalized wage rates depends on the relative size of the groups of high-wage and low-wage workers. Given the numbers of people now in the two groups, such equalization of wage rates would bring a great fall in the wage level and the standard of living of the United States and other high-income nations. The fact that some large, low-wage nations have very high rates of population-growth tellingly affects the future prospects of nations that are economically merged with these nations by international trade and wage-competition.

In theorizing, or thinking about the world in terms of words or conventionalized "models," one may assume that, say, "free trade is free trade," and it will have the same effects in one case as another. Thinking in terms of "principles" tempts us to neglect the influence on events of changing circumstances. In truth, a revolutionary change in conditions implies that "free trade" now has effects very different than in the past. The world now faces the challenge of dealing with a problem that has not existed in the past, and that can be understood only by escaping from traditional slogans, theories, and viewpoints.

3

WAGE-COMPETITION AND ITS IMPLICATIONS

To achieve trade policies that will make international trade a force for human betterment and will not undercut the standard of living of high-income nations requires an understanding of the processes that determine the effects of trade across national boundaries. The matter is considered further in this chapter.

THE RULE OF "ONE PRICE" AND THE FALL IN THE WEST'S STANDARD OF LIVING

The rule of "one price" generally applies where trading can occur. Within an open-trading area, a good tends to sell everywhere for the same price. For example, if barriers that prevented trade between Countries A and Z were removed the price of apples in the two countries would become the same. This would be true even though when the nations were separate and noncompeting areas the price of apples had been much higher in Country A. In the new situation, after all, who would pay more for Country-A apples, when they are identical to Country-B apples?

Wage rates in the two nations follow the same rule. Suppose Country-A workers had earned much higher wage rates when the two nations were separate, noncompeting areas. When the nations are economically merged through unrestricted trade, labor will come to have the same price in both areas. Workers of different skills and abilities still will earn different incomes, for they will continue to be noncompeting groups. But the wage differential associated with being a resident of Country A rather than Country B will end.

The equalization of wage rates will benefit the people of the low-wage nation, whose wage rate will rise. It will damage the people of the high-wage nation, whose wage rate will fall. How much the one wage will rise and the other fall will depend on the relative sizes of the two populations. If the low-wage nation is much the larger, the equalized wage rate will be close to its low initial wage rate. In this case, the high-wage nation will suffer a large reduction in its wage rate and standard of living.

This is a conventional economic analysis of the determination of competitive price by supply and demand. This conventional analysis seems quite valid.[1] The recent shift of industries and jobs from high-wage to low-wage nations illustrates its accuracy. A firm will not pay high wages for a job it can have done by a low-wage worker, any more than a person will pay a high price for apples when they can be bought for a low price. Competition among firms will force them to seek out the cheapest labor available—whether or not this is what the owners or managers would like to do.

WHAT DETERMINES WHETHER WORKERS ARE COMPETING OR NONCOMPETING GROUPS?

What determines whether wage-competition across national boundaries prevails, say, between the United States and China—and thus whether the rule of one price, i. e., of one wage rate, does or does not apply? One obvious way in which wage-

---

[1] In the literature of economics, this tendency of international trade to bring about a single price or income level for the various "factors of production" such as labor, capital, and land is expressed by "the factor-price equalization theorem." But this literature does not bring out the far-reaching implications of such equalization of wage rates and standards of living.

competition could prevail across two nations is for them to have "free migration," or the free movement of people. In the absence of "barriers to population movement," people would act in such a way as to bring about equalization of wage rates and living standards. People would move from the low-wage nation to take better-paid jobs in the high-wage nation. This movement of people would raise the wage in the low-wage nation and lower the wage in the high-wage nation. Such migration would tend to occur until the wage rates in the two countries were made equal.

As a matter of fact, this kind of movement of people, both legally and illegally, from lower-wage nations to take jobs in higher-wage nations is an important feature of the present-day world, and a problem for a number of nations. Not only the United States and Europe are suffering such an influx of people. India, for example, is subject to illegal immigration from nations with a still lower standard of living and worse unemployment that it suffers.[2]

Nations do not accept any principle of "free migration." It is widely understood that for a nation to permit unlimited immigration—in a world with billions of low-wage workers and hundreds of millions of unemployed or only partially employed workers—would invite an influx of people that could radically reduce its wage rate and standard of living.

But it is not so well understood that wage-competition across two nations will occur if industries and jobs are free to move to the low-wage nation, with the goods shipped back for sale in the markets of the high-wage nation. Workers in the lower-wage nation can take away the jobs of workers in the higher-wage nation as effectively by the jobs moving to them as by them moving to the jobs. Either way, the workers of what had been the higher-wage nation are thrown into wage-competition

---

[2] What the United States has been reluctant to do on its border with Mexico, India is doing, building "a 1,365-mile barbed-wire fence along its border with Bangladesh in an effort to prevent illegal immigration." "India to Proceed with Fence on Border with Bangladesh," *New York Times*, September 16, 1984, p. 8.

with those of the lower-wage nation. If the workers in both countries are available to do the same kinds of work and do it equally well, there will tend to be one, equalized wage rate.

Under "free trade" that permits goods produced in low-wage nations to be sold in the markets of high-wage nations, production will tend to shift from high-wage to low-wage nations. This shift will be forced on firms by competition among them. To avoid being undersold by other firms and failing, firms will have to shift production to the area where wages are lowest. Thus, workers in what had been the high-wage nation find their jobs disappearing. They will not be able to find anyone who will hire them at their accustomed level of wages. To regain employment, they will sooner or later have to accept jobs at the new "competitive wage," the one that results from their being put into wage-competition with the workers of the low-wage nation.

Such shifting of production and jobs to low-wage nations depends on the existence of "free trade." So long as the workers of the low-wage nations produce only for their home market, they are not undercutting the wages and taking the jobs of workers in the high-wage nation. The workers in the two nations are operating as noncompeting groups. And there would be little shifting of production from high-income to low-income nations if the goods could not be shipped back for sale in the large markets of the high-income nations. Computer firms would not move their production from the United States to Malaysia if they had to sell the output in Malaysia.[3]

What "free trade" does is to bring about a situation that from a common-sense viewpoint is somewhat strange. It puts the competing firms in a position in which, seemingly, they can "have their cake and eat it too." They can produce the goods cheaply in the low-wage nation, and can sell them in the attractive markets of the high-wage nation.

But, of course, this will not work out. When they have eaten their cake, they will find that they no longer have it, after all.

---

[3] The situation is more complicated in the case of production for the markets of a third country. For example, production of machinery for sale in Europe could shift from the U. S. to, say, South Korea *even though the United States did not permit unregulated imports.* The way cases of this type would work out under different trade policies needs careful analysis.

Shifting production and jobs out of the high-wage nation will shrink its incomes and markets. The rise in incomes in the low-wage nation, depending on its population situation, may do little to fill the gap. There the firms will be, with their nice, cheap goods to sell in high-income markets, and no high-income markets—all dressed up, and no place to go.

The recent discussion of international trade has neglected the indirect effects of trade, and its effects on the complex processes of economic change. Certain benefits of trade are played up, but the adverse effects of the trade are ignored. It is necessary to analyze *all* of the effects to determine what arrangements for trade actually will work to the benefit of the peoples of the nations involved, and mankind in general.

CLEARING UP A CONFUSION: "THE PRODUCTIVITY OF THE AMERICAN WORKER"

Some readers of the preceding pages will have wanted to raise this objection: "But didn't those high-wage United States workers have high wages because they had *high productivity*? And weren't the wages of the low-wage workers low because they had *low productivity*? How can low-productivity workers undercut the wages of high-productivity workers?"

This is a circular argument. It is *assumed* that workers with high wage rates *must have high "productivity,"* and those with low wages *must have low "productivity,"* in some ill-defined meaning of "productivity." Using the word, "productivity," in this way appears to "explain" and to validate whatever pattern of wages exists. Thus, it serves the purposes of *laissez faire* beliefs, seeming to show that "whatever is, is what ought to be." If one makes the additional assumption that this "productivity" is somehow built into the workers, so that it cannot be lost or disappear, then it seems that, in general, low-wage labor cannot undercut the incomes of high-wage labor.

In actuality, the wage rate any group of workers can earn depends on *the value of what they produce* (on their marginal value product, for readers familiar with these terms). And the value of the product, and thus of their work, can be radically and quickly changed by circumstances—such as being thrown into competition with low-wage labor. If American auto workers earning $12 an hour become subject to competition from Korean workers earning $1.25 an hour for working in the same kind of factories, the cheap imported cars will undersell the American-produced cars. The price at which American-made cars can be sold will drop. Then American cars can be sold at a competitive price only by using workers who are getting $1.25 an hour. It is *take wage cuts or lose your jobs*, a familiar refrain of the 1980s.

If the same production methods are being used in both countries, the "productivity" of the American labor falls, in the simplest case, from $12 an hour to $1.25 an hour. That is what American labor is worth to produce automobiles under the new set of circumstances. Subjecting high-wage workers to competition from low-wage workers can abruptly cut their productivity, the value of what they produce, and require them to accept a drop in wages to hold their jobs.

The American public and economists seem to have come to believe in the 1950s that American workers could do things that workers of other nations were simply incapable of doing. The reason Americans were the only workers producing automobiles and electrical appliances in large volume, they seemed to believe, was *because they were the only ones who were capable of producing them*. Possessed of this unique "productivity," American workers were not vulnerable to competition. For them, there could be no competing groups. They were above the competition of mere nonAmericans.

But when the aftermath of the Second World War disappeared, experience quickly showed that Europeans could do the same things that Americans could do, and so could Japanese, and Taiwanese, and Koreans, and Chinese. Workers throughout the world have shown themselves quite capable of working on the same kind of assembly lines that American workers worked on and of turning out the kinds of goods that American workers can turn out.

In truth, the United States automobile industry, for example, was unique not because American *workers* had unique abilities but because the United States had the first mass market for

Wage-Competition and Its Implications 27

automobiles—because it was the leading high-income nation. In this set of circumstances, the power of their labor union gained American auto workers wage rates that were high even in relation to average American wages. The high-priced cars produced with this high-priced labor could be sold in the great U. S. market and abroad because substantial production facilities for automobiles in other nations did not exist. Americans could get jobs at high wages (and had high "productivity" in *some sense* of "productivity") because they were making products that were in strong demand *and there was little competitive production*.

When American equipment, production techniques, and management methods are applied to producing automobiles using low-wage labor in other countries, the low-priced autos produced with the low-wage foreign labor undersell American production in world markets and in the U. S. market. Low-priced cars produced with low-wage labor undersell high-priced cars produced with high-wage labor. American production is cut back. American workers lose their jobs.[4]

The interpretation of "the productivity of the American worker," in economics textbooks and public discussion thus has been misleading. It misled people as to the effects of "free trade" under today's conditions—and kept people from understanding the effects of "free trade" and international wage-competition even as these were displayed before their eyes.[5]

---

[4] Such a shift of industries between nations need involve no net increase in world output, even in the short run. The one area applies more advanced technology and improves its position; the other one loses advanced-technology industries and jobs—high-paid steelworkers take new jobs as low-paid custodians. The balance of immediate gains and losses in the nations involved and the full effects of the change in the structure of economic activities are not predetermined by any principle, but must be analyzed in terms of the circumstances of each case. Even when there is a net advance in the technical level of production methods, this does not necessarily mean that people are made better off.

[5] A straightforward application of marginal productivity analysis to the case of competing and noncompeting groups leads to the kind of interpretation given here. The vocabulary and tools of economic analysis have been misused in support of "free trade" and *laissez faire* economic policies.

ANOTHER CONFUSION: "THE PRINCIPLE OF COMPARATIVE ADVANTAGE"

The early economists understood that workers in different parts of a country will tend to have the same level of wages. Thus, the opening of trade between a hitherto isolated high-wage South England and a low-wage North England would tend to equalize their wage rates. North England's wages would rise as it gained industries and jobs. South England's loss of industries and jobs would force it to accept a decline in its wage rate to the new competitive level.

But consider now the opening of unregulated trade between a high-wage England and, for example, a low-wage Portugal. The question that obviously arises is, "Why would England want to open 'free trade' with Portugal, when the effect will be to throw English workers into wage-competition with low-wage Portuguese workers, cause the loss of English industries and jobs, and reduce the nation's standard of living? Would not England be better off to avoid such an economic merger with Portugal?"

For Adam Smith, the rub was that for "free trade" to be harmful to England did not fit in at all with his faith in natural-harmony individualism. To rescue his political doctrine, Smith had to claim that unregulated international trade does not cause wage-competition and pull down the wages of high-wage nations. To justify this assertion, he had to claim that *international trade works basically differently than trade within a nation,* so that low-wage labor undercuts high-wage labor in trade within a nation but not in international trade.

The justification for this claim offered by Adam Smith and later David Ricardo was that trade in the two cases worked differently because capitalists would be willing to shift their investment from one area to another within England *but would not be willing to invest in a foreign country.*[6]

---

[6] See Adam Smith, *The Wealth of Nations* (New York: Random House, 1937, first published in 1776), especially pp. 421-425; and David Ricardo, *Principles of Political Economy and Taxation* (Harmondsworth, England: Penguin Books, 1971, first published in 1817), pp. 152-161.

This justification proves not to be acceptable, on two grounds. First, as a matter of fact, it is not generally true that capitalists are unwilling to invest abroad. Investment in foreign countries was occurring on a large scale by the 19th century, and recently has been a flood.

Second, even if it existed, an unwillingness of capitalists to invest abroad would not prevent a low-wage nation from undercutting the production of a high-wage nation. Low-wage Portugal (to take Ricardo's famous illustration) could use its cost advantage to undersell English goods in their home market *and the Portuguese capitalists could expand production out of the profits of their booming sales.* Smith's argument required that Portuguese production be able to undersell English production only if British capital moved to Portugal. This obviously is not correct. After all, the great Japanese industrial expansion in recent decades, which permitted Japanese output to undersell American output on a huge scale, was not based on American capital.

Recent textbooks continue to claim that trade across national boundaries works differently than other trade. Trade within a nation is agreed to be governed by "absolute advantage" or "absolute cost." Low-cost goods undersell high-cost goods, and cheap labor undersells dear labor. But international trade is said not to be affected by differences in absolute costs. It is asserted to depend only on "comparative advantage" rather than "absolute advantage." In other words, differences in the general levels of wages in the two nations have no effects at all. The recent international movements of industries specifically in pursuit of low labor costs refute "the principle of comparative advantage."

Economics textbooks now support "the principle of comparative advantage" by considering only hypothetical examples in which *the trade between the high-wage and the low-wage nation is in balance.* If the trade is in balance, the industries of the high-wage country cannot shift production to low-wage nations and ship the output back home to sell. The assumption that trade between the nations is in balance thus permits evasion of the whole problem of the international shifting of industries and jobs, and of international wage-competition.

In actuality, trade in such cases ordinarily will not be in balance. The shifting of industries and jobs to the low-wage nation throws the trade out of balance. The high-wage nation buys from the low-wage nation, but is unable to sell to it—until its wage level and standard of living have sufficiently declined. So this conventional textbook argument is misleading. Proving that absolute cost and differences in wage levels do not affect international trade by using only examples in which *the trade is in balance* is like proving that bullets do not kill by using only examples in which the bullets are made of marshmallow.

But people who take economics courses seem to learn "the principle of comparative advantage" all too well. Their hard-earned, though false, "knowledge" makes them unable to see what otherwise would be obvious—that the undercutting of high-wage production by low-wage foreign production is now drastically reshaping the human world.

The clarification of these influential errors serves to bring out some important points. Remembering that the "productivity" and the wage rate of the American worker is not built into the worker but depends critically on circumstances alerts us to the importance of maintaining those circumstances that will support a high standard of living for the nation. A major thing to be avoided is throwing American workers into wage-competition with large numbers of efficient low-wage workers in other countries.

And when they are correctly interpreted, the illustrations offered in economics textbooks to support "the principle of comparative advantage" bring out the importance of keeping international trade in balance. Doing this prevents—or at least limits—wage-competition, by preventing an unbalanced shift of production to low-wage nations.[7]

The arguments and illustrations that are used to claim that "free trade" is the best possible arrangement thus do not stand

---

[7] Again, this is true of direct trade between two nations. The case of a low-wage nation underselling the exports of a high-wage nation to other countries is an important and more complex case. Some discussion of this matter is given in Culbertson, *International Trade and the Future of the West* (Madison, Wis.: 21st Century Press, 1984), Chapters 4, 7.

critical examination. The reality is almost the opposite of the picture presented by the economics textbooks. Unregulated trade across national boundaries directly tends to pull wage levels and economic standards down to a lowest common denominator level. When indirect effects are taken into account, the hazards appear even greater, as we see in the next chapter.

4

FURTHER EFFECTS OF ECONOMIC MERGER

When the economic merger of nations through "free migration" or "free trade" moves their wage levels and standards of living toward equality, this change in the situation then has further consequences. The effects of one set of causes become the causes of another stage of effects. To understand the situations created by different arrangements for international trade, it is necessary to trace out these processes of change, to see in what direction they actually would take mankind.

DIFFICULTIES IN QUICKLY REDUCING A NATION'S STANDARD OF LIVING

For a nation quickly and efficiently to adapt to a lower standard of living is not easy, indeed, not possible. There thus is little truth in the common assertions that if everyone would buckle down and take the bitter medicine, all would be well. A *family* can quickly reduce its standard of living, sell the car and television, move to small and cheap quarters where mass transit is available. But what one family can do, the nation as a whole cannot do. Everyone cannot move to inexpensive housing, for not enough of it exists—the over-all stock of housing cannot be quickly changed. In nations that have become dependent on automobiles for transportation, it is not possible for most people to get to jobs and stores without a car. Neither is it possible to create at reasonable cost a public transportation system that will connect the scattered factories and stores of the automobilized nation.

To live at a low standard of living requires a particular pattern of life: inexpensive kinds of housing and buildings, locations of activities that permit cheap transportation, a low-cost kind of health care. Thus a society that has long experienced a high standard of living cannot be quickly transformed into an efficient low-income society, one that can compete on equal terms with nations adapted from long experience to a low-income pattern of life. And the conflicts, and even disorder, that commonly would be caused by the painful drop to a lower standard of living would pose further problems.

EFFECTS ON THE WORLD OF THE LOSS OF HIGH-INCOME NATIONS

The undercutting and disappearance of high-income nations would affect the future course of all nations. For one thing, the loss of high-income societies would drastically reduce the demand for the output of what have been the attractive industries—and the migrating industries—of recent years. The production of autos, say, shifts to South Korea and China, which undercuts American production and incomes, and then it turns out that there no longer is much of a market for autos. Many goods, and the technology that is used to produce these goods, would become obsolete in a world in which no large group of people had incomes high enough to buy them. With the shift back down to simpler and more basic consumer goods, recent "technological progress" would be reversed. Many of its innovations were geared to a high-income world, and would be useless in a low-income world.

Another kind of effect of the loss of high-income nations would be the cutback in research and development, and in scientific capabilities. Some kinds of technological know-how would remain relevant —indeed, essential—to the new low-income world. The population situation requires the knowledge and the technical and organizational capabilities lying behind the flow of chemical fertilizers, insecticides, genetic improvement of food plants and animals, and the capability to keep ahead of the evolving diseases and pests that threaten the food supply. These have been achievements of the well organized, high-income nations, which could and did carry their overhead costs and meet their demanding organizational requirements. The loss of these capabilities because of poverty and disorder would have dire consequences.

IMPLICATIONS OF MAKING THE WORLD A POPULATION COMMUNE

In throwing the people of different nations into wage-competition with one another, "free trade" or "free migration" would have the effect of making these nations a population commune. With world wage rates equalized, a situation would be created in which the standard of living and the effective degree of overpopulation of a nation did not depend on *its* behavior and *its* situation, but on the average population situation of the whole world.

This arrangement has the characteristic faults of the commune. The individual, and in this case the nation, has no hope of benefitting from constructive actions, achievements. Each is held down by the mass performance, within an incentive-framework in which the mass performance can hardly be anything but unfavorable. In other words, this is a structure the almost inevitable effect of which is to inflict on all of humanity the burdens of severe overpopulation. Universal overpopulation-caused poverty is its expected outcome.

It is illuminating to see that an overpulated nation can, if other nations permit it, quickly escape from the burden of its overpopulation—by imposing the burden equally on other nations. Obviously the overpopulated nation could physically impose its excess people on other nations through their emigration. But it could achieve the same effects by gaining the manufacturing industries and jobs of other nations through wage-competition. The wage-equalization this causes implies that the wage-depressing effects of the overpopulation would sit equally on all nations. The overpopulated nation now is no worse off than other nations.

Recent investigations in biology have disclosed that the higher animals achieve limitation of their populations and preservation of their habitats through arrangements that are territorial, that associate a particular group with a piece of territory. This permits a constructive competition or selection among groups. The group that permits overpopulation and destroys its habitat and its food supply does not survive; the group that limits its population and protects its habitat thrives, and becomes the pattern-setter for the species. The popular ideas of "one world," and "abolition of all boundaries and all groups" thus clash not only with the lessons of economic experience but also with the logic of constructive evolution among living things in general.

The earlier economists accepted the seemingly inescapable lesson of experience that except where some particular causes prevent this, population growth will tend to outrun possible increases in food production and force the wage rate down the "the subsistence level," at which poverty and disease raise the death rate and check the population growth. Adam Smith accepted this view, inconsistent though it was with his natural-harmony ideology.

These economists took for granted that a nation would not impose poverty on its people by accepting an influx of people from overpopulated nations. But, as we have seen, some of them were impelled by their *laissez faire* faith to argue that international trade worked differently than international migration—and differently than intranational trade. It is understandable that they should make this error, but somewhat surprising that the error should impel the late-twentieth-century United States to follow policies that invite its economic ruin.

IN A CAUSE-AND-EFFECT WORLD, STRUCTURE DETERMINES OUTCOME

The world of economically independent nations and the world as a population commune represent two kinds of systems or structures, which lead to two different evolutionary processes. A choice between types of economic structure is what basically is in question in the determination of rules for international trade. If the nations preserve their independence and their effectiveness as units for organizing economic activities (and other aspects of human life, such as environmental preservation), the nations can be the vehicles for the kind of constructive, follow-the-leader, or follow-the-success pattern that has been the source of human advancement down through history. This is the hopeful, if-anyone-succeeds-we-all-succeed type of structure. In the sixteenth century, other nations advanced by copying from the pace-setting Netherlands, later from England, then Germany, the United States, Japan.

This is an economic structure that permits, encourages, human economic progress. Its logic corresponds to that of constructive learning, and of the natural selection that underlies the development of all living things. The successes spread and prevail; the failures, in one way or another, drop out of the picture. This is the pattern that governs the effective competitive economy. Experience shows that it works.

But in an economically merged world, it is the failures that determine the outcome. The failures inflict the results of their failure, in redundant population, on the nations that otherwise could have been successes, and make them failures also. The power of population-growth is quite great enough to make failures of all nations. This kind of structure, then, tends to generate universal failure, to pull all down.[1]

"FREE TRADE"—*FREEDOM* OR *TYRANNY?*

Unregulated trade across national boundaries has been represented by its proponents as "free trade," as exemplifying "freedom," as a fundamental right of the kind that underlay the

---

[1] The constructive-competitive approach does not imply that other nations cannot try to help a failing nation to deal with its difficulties, or to become a success. But it will help no one for an effective nation to merge itself with an ineffective one in such a way that they both become ineffective. To be in a position to help other nations, either by example or in other ways, a nation must itself be a success, which it can be only by retaining its separateness and its control over its own affairs.

American Revolution. Is this a reasonable and accurate way to think about the matter?

The "freedom" that was the goal of the American Revolution was *freedom of the nation from outside control*, the freedom, or the power, of the people of the nation through their government to choose a course of development and pursue it, to make their own destiny. *The Declaration of Independence* was a declaration of the *independence* of the United States from outside dominance.

This nation-oriented conception of freedom conflicts with the individual-oriented, or anarchistic, conception of freedom, in which individuals and firms are to be free from outside influence, including the influence of the government of the nation. If individuals and firms can do as they like, and the national government cannot pass laws or regulations that guide and limit their actions, the nation has no capabilities.

"Free trade" gives to individuals and firms a power that undermines the independence of the nation, that merges it economically with other nations and deprives it of control over its own destiny. "Free trade" thus confers on traders privileges that undermine the "freedom" of the nation, and of its people. The people that are trapped in the destructive competition of an international economic commune can suffer a "tyranny" enormously more debilitating and degrading, surely, than anything the American colonists ever experienced at the hands of England. Indeed, this is perhaps the ultimate loss of independence and of the freedom that depends on independence, the ultimate tyranny.

5

ACHIEVING BENEFICIAL INTERNATIONAL TRADE

To achieve mutually beneficial trade between nations, two major problems must be solved. First, wage-competition and other types of degenerative competition must be prevented. This is largely achieved by arranging for the international trade (or trade plus approved credit) to be in balance. The balance in trade prevents low wage rates from undercutting high wage rates, and prevents other forms of antisocial cost-cutting from being spread by international competition.

Second, the pattern of international trade and the international location of industries must be arranged in a reasonable way, one that limits destructive competition among nations contending for jobs and the desirable industries of the times.

Unregulated profit-seeking trade across national boundaries under today's conditions will cause international wage-competition and other kinds of destructive competition. It will tend to drag all nations downward to a lowest common denominator level of living.

BALANCED TRADE; INTERNATIONAL TRADE AS TRADE BETWEEN *NATIONS*

In monitoring their international trade, the national governments will arrange for the trade to reflect a *balance*. A high-wage nation would not accept an unbalanced influx of imports that caused the loss of its industries and jobs to low-wage nations. An industrializing nation would not permit an influx of manufactured goods from industrialized nations that would prevent its manufacturing firms from ever getting started. When it is arranged by national governments, trade across national boundaries can be made to work like other trade, to be balanced and mutually beneficial.

In making such deals, each national government can protect its people against the particular hazards to which they are subject, while getting a *quid pro quo* for the particular trading assets the nation possesses. Their low-cost operations will be a trading asset to low-wage nations. Their large markets for advanced goods will be a trading asset to high-income nations. Nations have different trading assets that reflect their special capabilities and natural resources. The mutually beneficial economic deals that can be struck between nations fit in with the general working of the market or exchange economy. Such mutually beneficial, balanced deals permit specialization, division of labor, and technical efficiency. This system also preserves the independence and the effectiveness of nations, and thus preserves the if-anyone-succeeds-we-all-succeed structure of human life.

The actual management or guidance of their international trade by governments can be carried out through various kinds of actions. May kinds of trade-affecting actions now are being taken by governments.[1] What is lacking is an over-all frame-

---

[1] On this, see *The United States in a Changing World Economy: The Case for an Integrated Domestic and International Commercial Policy*, Staff Report of the Committee on Energy and Commerce, U. S. House of Representatives, September 1983, p. 34. This valuable report describes the melange of trade policies that now exist, proposes a basis for a new kind of trade policy, and offers illustrative proposals for actions.

work and logic that can make these actions mutually rewarding, rather than destructively competitive. And for each nation it is essential that a positive policy toward trade and industry be conceived and understood as a whole, rather than as a series of *ad hoc* responses to particular pressures.

A comprehensive, positive trade policy can offer a number of kinds of new rewards: (1) It can control the wage-competition and other kinds of destructive competition of the "bidding war" among nations seeking industries and jobs.

(2) It can keep the world from operating as a population commune, a structure in which high birth rates and overpopulation anywhere in the world drag all nations downward to poverty.

(3) It can remove the bias of the "free trade" framework against high-income nations by permitting their large markets for advanced goods to be a bargaining counter in international negotiations—rather than making them "sitting ducks" for the wage-competition and standards-competition of low-wage nations. As the counterpart of this, it can provide a framework that will help the less industrialized nations limit invasive competition by the technically advanced nations.

(4) It will make possible the formulation of beneficial packages of trade between nations of kinds that could not be carried out by private parties, with their narrower interests and viewpoints, more limited resources, and inability to implement important ones of the relevant *quid pro quos.*

ARRANGING THE PATTERN OF TRADE; WHICH NATION GETS WHICH INDUSTRIES?

Other nations have not been willing, and will not be willing, to leave to "the free market" the determination of which industries fall to which nations. If the United States attempts to play by free-trade rules when other nations are guiding their trade, it will tend to get the industries other nations do not want; it will be a self-made loser at the trade-and-industries game. But competitive, self-serving national actions taken unilaterally will lead to wasteful and destructive competition among nations for desired industries. There seems no reasonable course but to seek mutually advantageous deals between nations, and among groups of nations.

Such trade deals among governments unquestionably involve potential problems. Some governments may not fulfill their obligations, but this same difficulty is managed in deals between business firms. Governments that are realistic and competent will make out better than those that are not, but this is true in all kinds of activities.

Responsible and reasonable governments could work out kinds of mutually rewarding economic deals that could not be achieved in any other way. It may be that such positive international economic collaboration is the only feasible way to deal with the threats to the environment posed by modern technology. But the decisive consideration perhaps is that when the effects of "free trade" are accurately analyzed, and when the behaviors of other nations are realistically viewed, it becomes clear that there is no consructive alternative.

OTHER IDEAS AND PROPOSALS

What is the role of "industrial policy" in reasonable arrangements for international trade? "Industrial policy" in the sense of some positive guidance by government of the nation's trade and the structure of its industry seems to be a necessary element in any reasonable program of economic policy. But for Western nations to apply an "industrial policy" copied after the one that was so successfully used by Japan is a very different matter. Japan could "target" rewarding industries and win them away from Western nations because Japan could undersell the Western nations, because of its lower wage levels and the achievements of its government, firms, and labor. Since it could win the industries it chose, it made sense for Japan to decide which ones it most wanted to win.

But for a high-wage Western nation whose products are being undersold by efficient, low-wage, foreign production to "target industries" and try to hang onto them by large subsidies or other costly government programs is a quite different kettle of fish. The great costs incurred in such hopeless ventures would impose a tax burden that would reduce further the general competitiveness of the nation and its future prospects. "Industrial policy" thus is not a panacea or a magic-working force, but an action that has to be adapted to the particular circumstances of the nation.

What, then, of the view that "the smokestack industries" the United States has been losing are now in any case passé, second class, that an "advanced" nation like the United States should be happy to pass these industries down to other, and lesser, nations, that it should move on to higher and newer things, to the exciting *new* industries of "the postindustrial era"? To Americans, this story is cheering, and flattering. But is it realistic?

This doctrine again makes the experience-refuted assumption that Americans can do things that people of other nations cannot do, so that those bright new industries, if they appeared, would fall to *us* rather than to the nations that recently have been undercutting us in existing industries. This is the productivity-of-the-American-worker fallacy again.

The doctrine also assumes that ballooning standards of living throughout the world are going to cause consumer goods such as radios and autos to become obsolete and replaced by esoteric and higher-tech goods whose production will provide tens of millions of new jobs. In truth, in few nations, if any, will living standards shoot up into a science-fiction range in the near future. The great mass of jobs will continue to be in the production of familiar types of goods, which fit the living standards nations are able to achieve under the existing circumstances.

Some Western governments see the answer to lost jobs and rising unemployment in *the retraining of workers*. But for such retraining to be helpful, rather than another kind of costly but useless political gesture, it must be based on a realistic answer to the question: "Retraining *to do what?* What kind of jobs will our workers continue to be able to hold against foreign competition?" Unless international trade is organized in a new way, the situation for which Western workers will need to be "retrained" may be one that their governments would hesitate to disclose to them.

PREVENTING CATASTROPHE; EVOLVING UPWARD

The economic future of the West and of all of mankind depends critically on the way international trade is structured in the years ahead. Already under way is a process of destructive competition that will tend to make nations impotent and leave mankind out of control, to impose overpopulation-caused poverty on all of mankind, to cause disorder and disintegration in nations afflicted with disappearing jobs and declining incomes, and to extinguish the knowledge and the technical and organizational capabilities that have been built up in the constructive evolution of the past—on which the existing way of life and the feeding of billions of people depends.

On the other hand, the knowledge and the technical and organizational capabilities that mankind has so augmented in recent decades provide the potential basis for exciting steps forward—*if human affairs can be so structured as to bring constructive, rather than destructive, competition and evolution.* International trade can be structured so as to bring to economic relations among nations the pattern of constructive, mutually beneficial dealings that prevails in successful economies and in the natural world. The basic challenge is to organize human beings so their future can be governed by their achievements and successes, rather than by their failures, and thus to cause mankind to be elevated, and civilized societies to be developed and preserved, by causing high human goals to be realized—in a universe that has demonstrated its indifference to human failure and degradation.

Most people's values would lead them to support the needed restructuring of international trade, once they accurately see the issues. The conservative does not want to destroy the nation as a unit of economic organization, to throw all of humanity into a vast, purposeless, out-of-control commune. The liberal does not want to nullify national governments and lose the potentiality for the kinds of reforms and positive governmental programs that comprise the liberal agenda. People habituated to slogans like "the free market" or "economic freedom" do not mean to support policies that lead to an economically merged world that is governed by a degrading competition to produce goods cheap by making people cheap.

The impediment to realistic actions, thus, seems to be not conflicts of basic values so much as unrealistic theories and ideas. The degree of success that is achieved in the years ahead in thinking realistically about international trade will importantly affect the human future.